FOCUS ON
INSECTS

CLASSIFICATION

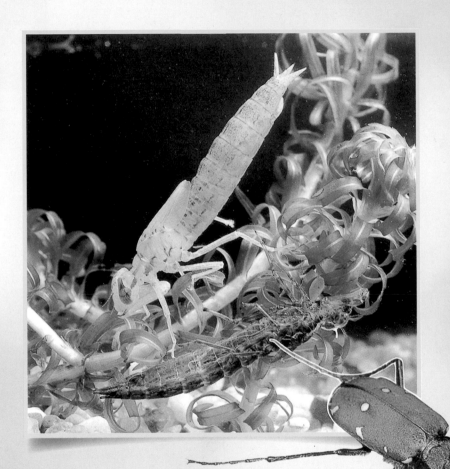

Stephen Savage

This edition published in 2014 by Wayland
Copyright © Wayland 2014

Wayland
338 Euston Road
London NW1 3BH

Wayland Australia
Level 17/207 Kent Street
Sydney, NSW 2000

Editor: Carron Brown
Designer: Alyssa Peacock

Dewey number: 595.7-dc23

ISBN 978 0 7502 8488 2

Printed in China

10 9 8 7 6 5 4 3 2 1

Picture acknowledgements: Bruce Coleman Ltd 26(lower), /M.P.L. Fogden 4, /Andrew Purcell 5, /David Hughes 6(top), /
Luiz Marigo 6(lower), /Kim Taylor 7, 9(top), /Andrew Purcell 9(lower), /Jenny Grayson 10(top), /Kevin Rushby 10
(lower), /Luiz Marigo 11(top), /Kim Taylor 11(lower), /Harold Lange 12, /Ingo Arnot 13(top), /Jeremy Grayson
13(lower), /Kim Taylor 14(top), /Janos Jurka 15, /Kim Taylor 15(inset), 16, /Leonard Lee Rue 17(top), /Andrew
Purcell 17(lower) and title page, /J. Brackenbury 18(top), /Kim Taylor 18(lower), Jens Rydell 19 and contents
page, /Jane Burton 20 and title page, /Kim Taylor 21, /Frieder Sauder 22, /Kim Taylor 23, /Jane Burton 25,
/Peter Evans 26(top), /Peter Hinchcliffe 26(lower); Discovery Books 24(lower); FLPA /B. Borrell cover (inset),
/Chris Mattison 14(lower); Oxford Scientifi c Films /David Dennis; Shutterstock, cover picture; Wayland Picture
Library 24(top). Artwork on pages 28-9 by Mark Whitchurch and on page 22 by John Yates.

First published in 2000 by Wayland

Wayland is a division of Hachette Children's Books, an Hachette UK company.
www.hachette.co.uk

Contents

What a difference!	4
Where insects live	6
Catching a meal	8
Hot and cold	12
Getting around	16
Insect young	20
Insect pets	24
Unusual insects	26
Scale of insects	28
Topic web	30
Activities	30
Glossary	31
Finding out more	31
Index	32

What a difference!

INSECT CHARACTERISTICS

- Insects have three parts to their body.
- Most insects have six legs.
- Insects have large compound eyes so that they can see all around.
- Most insects have wings.

There are more insects in the world than any other animal. They all have similar features but their size, colour and shape can be very different.

↓ The largest beetles are male Hercules beetles. With their giant horns, each of these two fighters measures almost 15 centimetres (6 inches) long.

The young of most insects do not look like their parents. They do not have wings and may have extra legs.

⬆ There are many beautiful butterflies and moths. This emperor moth, resting on a tree trunk, has false eye spots to confuse predators.

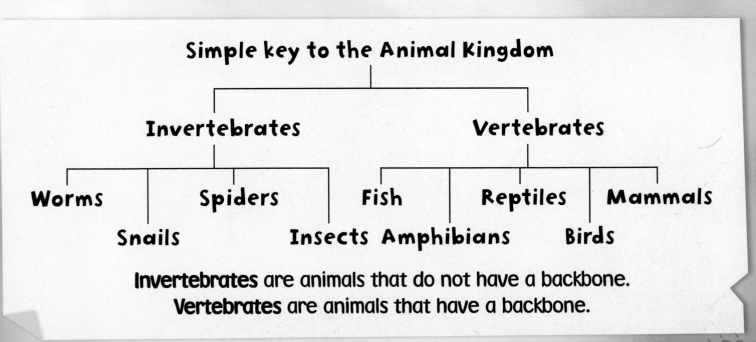

Simple key to the Animal Kingdom

Invertebrates   **Vertebrates**

Worms   Spiders   Fish   Reptiles   Mammals

Snails   Insects   Amphibians   Birds

Invertebrates are animals that do not have a backbone.
Vertebrates are animals that have a backbone.

Where insects live

Insects are found in many of the world's habitats. They live in forests, grasslands, mountains, deserts, lakes, rivers and ponds. They even live in towns and cities.

Insects have special features that help them cope with the problems of living in these very different places.

↑ Although the darkling beetle lives in the waterless desert, it obtains water from droplets that form on its body and run down to its mouth.

← The morpho butterfly feeds on the juices from overripe fruit in the South American rainforest.

DIFFERENT HABITATS

- Insects that live in grass are usually green or brown.

- Pond insects can fly from one pond to another.

- Field crickets lay their eggs underground.

- Desert ants collect and store seeds to eat when there is no other food.

The water boatman lives in ponds. It can breathe underwater because it carries an air bubble beneath its body.

Catching a meal

Some insects eat plants or drink the nectar from flowers. Caterpillars chew the leaves of plants. When they become adult butterflies or moths, most will sip nectar.

AVOIDING PREDATORS

- Some beetles squirt chemicals at an attacker.
- The caterpillar of a swallowtail butterfly looks like a bird dropping to put off predators.
- Eye spots on a moth or butterfly may frighten off an attacker (see page 5).

⬇ Leaf-cutter ants carry leaves back to the nest. The leaves make a garden that grows a special fungus that the ants eat.

Many insects are predators. They eat other insects and tiny animals, which they catch with large, powerful jaws. Huge numbers of army ants on the march can overwhelm insects, small mammals and birds because there are so many of them.

↑ This adult dragonfly waits to catch flying insects with its jaws.

← A green tiger beetle feeding on a caterpillar.

Insects are eaten by birds and mammals. To protect themselves, many insects are coloured to help them blend in with their surroundings. Some look exactly like sticks, leaves or plants.

The two yellow-and-black striped ➡ hoverflies feeding in the centre of the thistle look like wasps. Most insect-eating animals see the warning colours and keep away.

⬇ This praying mantis looks just like a flower. The disguise tricks its prey and also protects it from insect-eating mammals and birds.

↑ A katydid in the South American rainforest mimics a dead leaf so that other insect-eating animals will not recognise it and want to eat it.

Many insects, such as wasps, have a sting to protect them, or to paralyse other insects. Some may taste horrible. These types of insects are brightly coloured to warn other animals to stay away.

← This close-up picture of a housefly shows its compound eyes, which allow it to see an attacker even from behind.

Hot and cold

Insects are often active on sunny days but find shelter when it is cold. Many flying insects need to warm their wings before they can fly.

HOW TO KEEP WARM AND COOL

- Some hibernating insects have a chemical in their blood to prevent it from freezing.

- Mountain insects live at temperatures of around 0°C (32°F).

- Some moths' bodies are covered in hair to keep them warm.

- Compass termites in Australia build a wedge-shaped nest. The thin edge faces the sun to help keep it cool.

↓ This tortoiseshell butterfly is sunbathing. Many butterflies warm their wings in this way.

← These North American monarch butterflies, hanging from the branches of a tree, are preparing to migrate to warmer countries to breed. They migrate so their caterpillars will not be killed by winter frosts.

↓ Black ants move their developing young from one chamber to another. This keeps them at the right temperature.

Most ants live in underground nests made up of different chambers and tunnels. Some chambers are warmer than others.

On a hot summer's day, ground-living insects stay in the shade. Many desert insects come out only at night, to avoid the blazing sun.

← This beetle lives in the Kalahari Desert in Africa. It has long legs so that its body is kept off the scorching sand.

Worker honey → bees at the entrance to the hive. They sometimes fan their wings to help keep the hive cool.

Tiny, ant-like termites build special chimneys on the outside of their tall nests. This helps to keep the nest cool.

⬇ Termites in Africa build tall nests to allow air to circulate through the chambers. (Inset) Termites inside the nest.

Getting around

Most insects have wings. Butterflies and other flying insects use their wings to fly from place to place, or to escape from danger.

↑ Unlike butterflies that flutter, the hoverfly can hover in the air, or fly off at high speed.

Some types of insects walk or run, using their six legs. Their wings are covered by a hard wing case, ready to be opened when they are needed.

MOVING AROUND

- Some grasshoppers can leap 70 centimetres (28 inches).

- Water beetles can swim underwater.

- Some types of insects have two wings and others have four.

- Monarch butterflies fly several thousand kilometres when they migrate to breed.

↑ A stick insect climbing up the bark of a tree.

↓ A green tiger beetle can run 60 centimetres (24 inches) a second. This speed is equal to a large mammal running 400 kilometres (250 miles) per hour.

A few types of insect can walk on the surface of still water. They eat other insects that fall onto the surface.

The larvae of many insects are able to move around by wriggling or crawling.

Crickets and ➜ grasshoppers can leap huge distances to escape danger.

⬇ Pond skaters have special hairs on their legs that allow them to walk on water.

Caterpillars crawl with the help of ten legs. The flying adult will have only six legs.

Insect young

Insects use various ways to attract a mate. Grasshoppers, crickets and a few other insects make sounds. Some female insects produce a scent that attracts a male.

↓ Dragonflies lay their eggs in ponds. The larvae live in the water until they are ready to become adults. This dragonfly larva is in the final stage before it becomes an adult.

All insects lay eggs. Most types of insect lay hundreds of eggs, but only a few will survive to become adults.

↓ The dung beetle lays an egg on a dung ball that it has made from animal dung. The egg is buried with other dung balls, each in a special chamber.

LIFE CYCLE

- Insects lay eggs.
- Eggs hatch into larvae.
- Larvae become chrysalises (or pupae).
- Adult insects emerge from pupae.

Some insects take great care of their young. They will even defend them against predators much larger than themselves.

↑ A female shield bug protects her eggs and young with her shield-like body. The young bugs look just like their parents.

Life Cycle of a Butterfly

Mating

Adult butterfly

Emerging butterfly

Eggs

Caterpillar (larva)

Chrysalis (pupa)

Honeybee larvae develop within brood cells. They are protected by the rest of the bee colony.

Honeybees and ants live in large colonies ruled by a queen. Most of the colony is made up of workers who collect food and take care of the young.

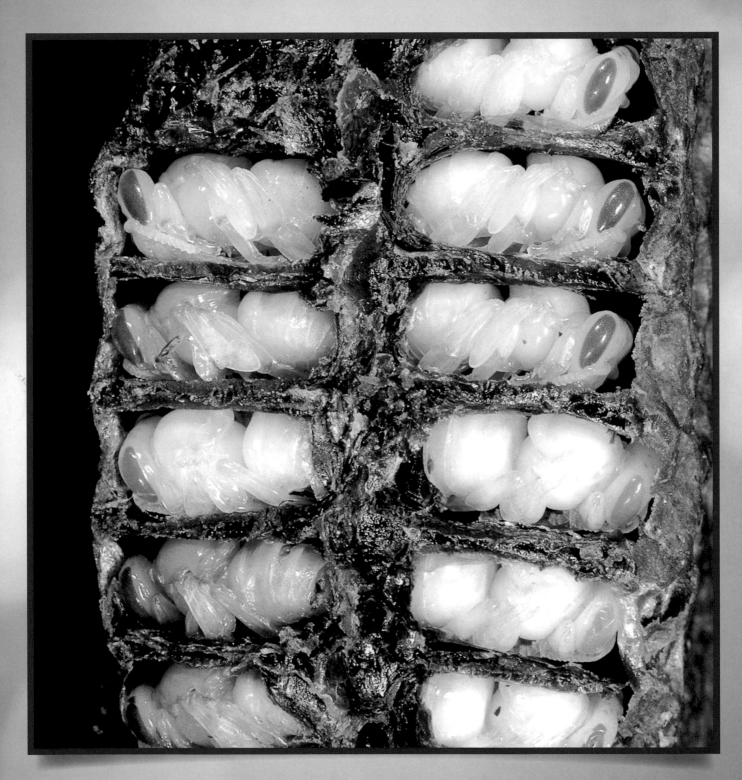

Insect pets

Not many insects make good pets. Your garden is the best place to watch insects, especially around plants and under stones and logs.

↓ Stick insects are sometimes kept as pets.

TAKING CARE OF INSECTS

- You need a tank with a lid and air holes.

- Provide the right food to eat.

- Give them twigs and foliage for climbing on.

- If you keep insects in an aquarium, you will need an air pump.

Many insects are attracted to gardens by flowers. They feed on their nectar and pollinate them with pollen from other flowers so they can reproduce. Insects and flowers need each other to survive.

↑ Keep caterpillars in a tank to watch them change, first into chrysalises and then into butterflies. This red admiral butterfly has emerged from its chrysalis.

Unusual insects

A few insects are among the most amazing creatures of the animal world. Some are very brightly coloured or have bodies that are very strangely shaped.

↑ The back end of the hawk moth caterpillar looks like the head of a snake. This frightens away most attackers.

← The bodies of some honey pot worker ants become honey stores, to feed the ant community when food is scarce.

The lives of some insects are so unusual that they appear strange even for insects.

↓ Chemicals inside a female glow-worm's body produce a light that attracts male glow-worms.

27

Scale of insects

| Human hand | Swallowtail butterfly | Morpho butterfly | Hercules beetle | Emperor moth | Dragonfly | Praying mantis |

| Human finger | Darkling beetle | Water boatman | Field cricket | Army ant | Leaf-cutter ant |

| Human finger | Black ant, worker | Honeybee, worker | Desert beetle | Termite, worker | Pond skater |

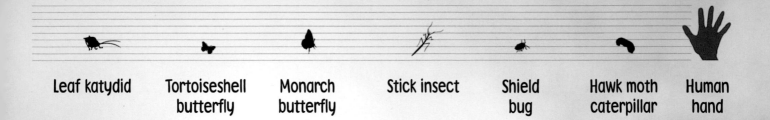

Leaf katydid   Tortoiseshell butterfly   Monarch butterfly   Stick insect   Shield bug   Hawk moth caterpillar   Human hand

Green tiger beetle   Grasshopper   Common wasp   Housefly   Housefly   Human finger

Swallowtail caterpillar   Dung beetle   Honey Pot ant   Glow-worm   Mosquito   Greenfly   Human finger

Topic web

SCIENCE
Classification.
Life cycles.
How insects adapt to their environment.
Food chains.
Predators and prey.

GEOGRAPHY
Insect habitats - forests, grasslands, deserts, mountains, rivers and ponds.

MATHS
Measure and compare different insects with each other.

ARTS & CRAFTS
Paint a mural showing different insects.
Make a life-cycle mobile.

DRAMA/DANCE
Mime the stages of a caterpillar changing into a butterfly.
Improvise dances to show the ways different types of insects move.

ENGLISH
Write about a day in the life of a chosen insect.

Activities

Science Look for mini creatures in your garden or school playground. Collect some of them and write down what you find out about them. Check the key on page 5 and decide which are insects (see also 'Characteristics' on page 4). Library books will help you to decide what groups the other mini creatures belong to.

Geography List the habitats in which various insects live. Look up the habitats in an atlas and draw a simple world map showing these habitats and which insects live in them.

Arts & Crafts Make a mobile showing the life cycle of a butterfly or moth. You can hang the chrysalis, caterpillar and egg at different heights from the adult.

English Write a diary entry describing a day in the life of a worker ant (or any insect of your choice). What does a worker ant do in a day: for example, collect food, care for the ant larvae or prepare the nest.

Drama/Dance Mime the life cycle of a butterfly - the egg, caterpillar, chrysalis, emerging butterfly and finally the adult, flying away. Create a dance to show how different insects move: for example, flying, crawling, running, leaping or swimming.

Maths Use the scale on pages 28-29 to compare the sizes of different insects with each other. Compare their sizes with the size of your hand or of your index finger. Are any of the insects bigger than your hand?

Glossary

Brood cells The chambers of a bees' nest or hive where the young develop.

Compound eyes The eyes of insects, which are made up of hundreds of tiny lenses.

Habitat The natural home of plants and animals.

Hibernate To spend the winter in a state similar to sleep.

Katydid A type of grasshopper found in North and South America.

Larvae Grubs or insects after they have left their eggs but before they become adults. A single grub is a larva. The larvae of butterflies and moths are called caterpillars.

Migrate To move from one region to another in search of food or a warmer climate.

Nectar A sugary substance produced by plants to attract insects.

Pollinate To fertilize plants and flowers with pollen so that they will produce seeds.

Predators Animals that hunt others for food.

Prey Animals that are hunted and killed for food.

Queen The fertile female in a colony of ants, bees or other similar insects.

Finding out more

Books to read

Extraordinary Bugs by Leon Gray (Wayland, 2011)

Explorers: Insects and Minibeasts by Jinny Johnson (Kingfisher, 2014)

Ultimate Bugopedia: The Most Complete Bug Reference Ever by Darlyne Murawski and Nancy Honovich (National Geographic Kids, 2013)

Wildlife Wonders: Why Do Insects Have Six Legs? by Pat Jacobs (Franklin Watts, 2014)

Websites

BBC
www.bbc.co.uk/nature/life/Insect/by/rank/all
Discover amazing facts and videos about insects from around the world.

Natural History Museum
www.nhm.ac.uk/kids-only/life/life-small/index.html
Read more about bees, cockroaches and butterflies.

Wildlife Watch
www.wildlifewatch.org.uk/explore-wildlife/animals/minibeasts
Find out which minibeasts live near you.

Index

Page numbers in **bold** refer to photographs.

aardvark **9**
animal kingdom key 5
ants 23
  ant colonies 23, 26
  ants' nest 8, **13**
  army ants 9
  black ants **13**
  desert ants 7
  honey pot ants **26**
  leaf-cutter ants **8**

bee colony **23**
beehive 14
bees (see honeybees)
beetles 8
  darkling beetle **6**
  desert beetle **14**
  dung beetle **21**
  green tiger beetle **9**, **17**
  Hercules beetles **4**
  water beetles 17
butterflies 5, 8, 16, 22, 25
  butterfly life cycle **22**
  monarch butterflies **13**, 17
  morpho butterfly **6**
  red admiral butterfly 25
  swallowtail butterfly 8
  tortoiseshell butterfly 6, **12**

caterpillars 8, 13, **19**, **25**, 26
  hawk moth caterpillar **26**

chrysalises 21, **25**
compound eyes 4, **11**
crickets 7, **18**, 20

desert 6, **14**
dragonfly **9**, **20**

eggs 7, 21, 22
eye spots **5**, 8

fleas 27
flowers 25
forests 6

glow-worms 27
grasslands 6
grasshopper 17, 18, 20
greenfly 27

habitats 6, 7
hibernating 12
honeybees **14**, 23
housefly **11**
hoverflies **10**, **16**

insect young 5, 20–23

katydid **11**

larvae 18, 20, **23**
legs 4, 17, 18

migrating 13, 17
mosquitoes 27
moths 5, 8, 12
  emperor moth **5**
mountain insects 12

nectar 8, 25
nests 8, 13, **15**

pond 6, 18, 20
pond skaters **18**
praying mantis **10**
predators 9, 22

queen bee 23

rain forest 6, 11

shield bug **22**
stick insects **17**, **24**

termites 12, **15**
termites' nest **15**

wasps 11
water boatman 7
wings 4, 12, 16, 17